WELCOME TO BA...
BIOGRAPHIES FOR KIDS

Paragon Publishing offers a wide selection of other sports biographies and quiz books, so be sure to check them out if you enjoy this one.

Paragon Publishing is a privately run publishing company which cares greatly about the accuracy of its content.

As many facts and figures in this book are subject to change, please email us at **ParagonPublishing23@gmail.com** if you notice any inaccuracies to help us keep our book as up-to-date and as accurate as possible.

Enjoy!

CONTENTS

INTRODUCTION

This book will take a look at the 25 greatest basketball players to ever play the great game. You will learn how each of these legends started playing basketball as a child, and then all the great things they achieved over their careers. Some of these athletes played a very long time ago, so there may even be names that you do not recognise, or do not know much about.

Before we delve into some of the greatest players to ever play basketball, let's take a brief look at its history, and how the game got to be where it is today. Basketball was invented by a man named James Naismith on or about December 1, 1891, at the International Young Men's Christian Association (YMCA) Training School in Springfield Massachusetts, where he was a teacher in physical education. Naismith used two half-bushel peach baskets as goals, which is where the sport got its name. This first game was won by William Richmond Chase, who made a midcourt shot, the only score in the contest.

Word spread about the game, and Naismith made the first copy of the rules on January 15, 1892. The number of players per team varied from 5-9 in the early days, but in 1897 the rules set it at 5. Basketball soon began to spread around the world, with it being introduced to France in 1893, England in 1894, and Australia, China and India soon after. In 1896 the points for making a basket was reduced from 3 to 2, and the points for making a free throw were reduced from 3 to 1.

Basketball was exploding at this point, and naturally, the first professional basketball league was formed in 1898. Six teams took part in the National Basketball League, with Trenton Nationals coming out on top in the first season.

The first international game of basketball took place in Saint Petersburg in 1909, with Mayak Saint Petersburg beating a YMCA American team. 23 years later, FIBA (Fédération internationale de basketball amateur) formed. This was the first real international basketball federation, helping basketball to appear in its first Olympics in 1936. The NBA soon formed on June 6, 1946, and the rest is history.

Basketball very quickly grew from a chaotic sport without clear rules to become one of the biggest sports the world has ever seen. Today it is estimated that 450 million people play basketball!

From all the millions of people who have ever played the game, this book has selected the 25 greatest players of all time. Being called one of the GOAT's (Greatest Of All Time) is a very big claim to make and there are many factors that must be ticked for a player to even be considered in this bracket. It is not just the number of baskets scored over their careers, or the number of Championships won, but it is also about their ability to be a great leader in the team, to step up in the big games, and to leave a legacy.

MICHAEL JORDAN

Full Name	Michael Jeffrey Jordan
Nicknames	Air Jordan, Black Cat
Main Position	Shooting Guard
Nationality	American
NBA Debut	1984
Height	1.98m or 6ft 6

CAREER

CHICAGO BULLS
1984-1993

⬇

CHICAGO BULLS
1995-1998

⬇

WASHINGTON WIZARDS
2001-2003

TROPHY CABINET

NBA Championship 🏆 X6

(1990-91, 1991-92, 1992-93, 1995-96, 1996-97, 1997-98)

All-Star Game	🏆 X14	Olympic Gold	X2
Season MVP	🏆 X5	Steals Leader 🏆	X3
Defensive Player of the Year	🏆 X1	Finals MVP 🏆	X6
Scoring Leader	🏆 X10		
All-NBA First Team	🏆 X10		
All-Defensive First Team	🏆 X9		
Rookie of the Year	🏆 X1		
All-NBA Second Team	🏆 X1		

EARLY CAREER

Michael Jeffrey Jordan was born in the borough of Brooklyn, New York, USA. His family moved to Wilmington, North Carolina, where Jordan played in a variety of sports at school. Jordan had to play in the junior basketball team due to his height at the time (5 foot 11). Jordan excelled and made his way into the varsity team before taking on a basketball scholarship in 1981. He won the Freshman of the Year award before attempting to gain a place in the 1984 NBA draft (National Basketball Association), and eventually graduated with a Bachelor of Arts degree in Geography.

Having gained his professional place with the Chicago Bulls in 1984, Jordan quickly became a fan favorite and effective all-round player despite his side losing in the early round of the playoffs. He became something of a sensation in 1985, when he shattered the backboard glass when executing a dunk in an exhibition game in Italy.

LATER CAREER

Jordan led the scoring stakes in the next few seasons before eventually helping the Bulls to three straight NBA titles between 1991 and 1993, and becoming the first player in history to win three MVP (Most Valuable Player) Finals awards in succession. A bout of gambling issues, the death of his father, and retirement from the sport followed, before trying his hand at minor league baseball. A sensational return to the NBA in 1995 saw more high-scoring from Jordan, before helping the Bulls to another three successive titles (1996-1998), aided by a certain Dennis Rodman along the way. Three more MVP Finals awards meant Jordan had a record-breaking six in total. A second retirement followed before coming back in an administrative role for the Washington Wizards in 2000. He played a few times for the Wizards in another comeback stint.

GREATEST ACHIEVEMENTS IN BASKETBALL

Apart from winning six NBA titles with the Bulls and numerous MVP awards, Jordan also won Defensive player of the year, Rookie of the year, several All-Star game awards, and the scoring champion stats on many occasions, along with countless other achievements. For the USA, he won two Olympic gold medals, and was inducted into several Halls of Fame, the first one in 2009. Jordan has been ranked at number one in various polls for his success during his basketball career, and in 2016, he received the Presidential Medal of Freedom. In 15 seasons, Jordan played 1072 games, and scored 32,292 points, at an average of 30.12 points per game. His main position was as a 'shooting guard'.

RETIREMENT

Michael Jordan has been just as successful off the court as on it. Advertising, ownership of sports teams, brand sponsorship, and a main role in the 1996 film Space Jam are just some of his many lucrative and highly prosperous ventures. He is currently the owner and chairman of NBA side Charlotte Hornets. It is estimated that his net worth is over one billion dollars.

SUMMARY

Michael Jordan's main strengths were in scoring points, defensive duties, and running the general play. He decided many games with his skills and used his short stature to become an all-round player in all aspects of the game. In charity work, Jordan has hosted golf tournaments, supported the 'Make-A-Wish Foundation' and donated towards helping people affected by natural disasters.

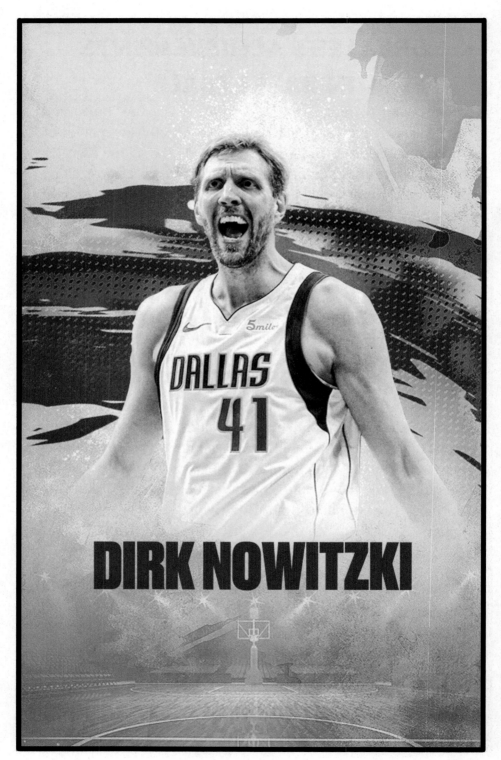

Full Name	Dirk Werner Nowitzki
Nicknames	The Germanator
Main Position	Power Forward
Nationality	German
NBA Debut	1999
Height	2.13m or 7ft 0

CAREER

DALLAS MAVERICKS
1998-2019

TROPHY CABINET

NBA Championship X1

(2010-11)

All-Star Game  X14

Season MVP x1

Finals MVP x1

All-NBA First Team x4

All-NBA Second Team x5

EARLY CAREER

Dirk Werner Nowitzki was born in the city of Wurzburg, West Germany. Both his mother and sister were basketball players, and his father competed in handball. He was extremely tall as a child, and played handball and tennis at school. He eventually joined the local sports club DJK Wurzburg when 15, and soon improved his game through the coaching from a former German basketball player.

Impressive performances in Germany's second tier basketball league saw Nowitzki take part in events involving other NBA stars. In 1998, he became only the fourth player from Germany to play in the NBA, when he was picked by the Dallas Mavericks. He struggled early on playing as a power forward against the more nimble and athletic NBA forwards.

LATER CAREER

However, the coming of billionaire Mark Cuban as the new owner in 2000 saw a reversal of fortunes for Nowitzki. He became the tallest player to take part in the three-point contest, and played all 82 games in 2000/01. He assisted the Dallas Mavericks to their first playoffs since 1990. The contract offered to him in 2001/02 made him the second highest paid German sportsperson after motor racing driver Michael Schumacher. In 2004, he accumulated 53 points in a game, a career-best, before recording the highest scoring average by a European player in a season in 2005/06.

High numbers in the playing stats earned Nowitzki the 2007 MVP award; the first European to win this. And in 2011, he scored the winning basket in game 4 of the Finals against Miami Heat, when suffering from a fever, as the Mavericks won their inaugural championship. He was the sixth player to reach 30,000 points in an NBA career; the first overseas international to do so. In his final home game in 2019 he notched up another 30 points, before announcing his retirement.

GREATEST ACHIEVEMENTS IN BASKETBALL

Nowitzki played his entire 21-year NBA career at Dallas Mavericks, making the playoffs 15 times. One NBA title, the MVP in Finals, and a points record of 31,560 points (average 20.7 per game), and 11,489 rebounds (7.5 per game), in 1522 games. He is the only player to have the distinction of the combined play statistic of 31,000 points, 10,000 rebounds, 3000 assists, 1000 steals, 1000 blocks, and 1000 three-point field goals. Outside the NBA, he was the top scorer at the 2002 FIBA World Championships, the German sports personality of the year in 2011, and he received the Laureus Lifetime Achievement award in 2020. His position was as a 'power forward' and 'center'.

RETIREMENT

Nowitzki is now a special adviser to the Dallas Mavericks. A film documentary was made celebrating his life and career. He is also a football association fan, being a supporter of Arsenal FC.

SUMMARY

Dirk Nowitzki has been considered as the greatest European player ever, playing as a center and power forward. His one-legged fadeaway jump shot has been described as one of the most unstoppable moves ever.

JULIUS ERVING

Full Name	Julius Winfield Erving II
Nicknames	Dr. J, Doctor
Main Position	Small Forward
Nationality	American
NBA Debut	1976
Height	2.01m or 6ft 7

CAREER

VIRGINIA SQUIRES (ABA)
1971-1973

NEW YORK NETS (ABA)
1973-1976

PHILADELPHIA 76ERS
1976-1987

TROPHY CABINET

NBA Championship X1

(1982-83)

Season MVP X1

All-NBA First Team X5

All-NBA Second Team 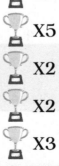 X2

ABA Championship X2

ABA Season MVP X3

EARLY CAREER

Julius Winfield Erving II was born in the district of East Meadow, in New York, before being raised in Roosevelt, New York, from his early teens. He got his nickname 'Doctor' and 'Dr J' from a high school friend, and attended the University of Massachusetts from 1968. As well as playing basketball, Erving earned a Bachelor degree in administration and creative leadership in 1986.

He joined the team of Virginia Squires in the ABA (American Basketball Association) in 1971, and soon developed into a forceful and hard player. After some toing and froing Erving went to the New York Nets in 1973, and helped them win their first ABA championship. He was seen as the most prominent player in the league at this time. The end of the 1975/76 season saw the merger between the ABA and the NBA.

LATER CAREER

The Philadelphia 76ers decided to take on Erving for the 1976/77 season, after the New York Knicks turned him down. Now seen as the leader, Erving helped the 76ers to be victorious in 50 games before losing in the finals. In game 6 of those Finals, he ran the full length of the court before slam dunking a basket over the defensive legend Bill Walton, despite having five defenders chasing him. He became a success off the court, endorsing products and starring in a film. In the 1980 Finals, Erving completed a legendary behind-the-board reverse lay-up dubbed the 'baseline move', and in 1981 was named the MVP.

With the admission of Moses Malone to the team in 1982/83, Erving won his first NBA title. Aged 37, he played his final game in 1987, and due to his popularity and stature, he received a tribute by opposing teams on his farewell appearances.

GREATEST ACHIEVEMENTS IN BASKETBALL

In a combined career in both the NBA and ABA, Erving played in 1243 games, and scored 30,026 points, at an average of 24.2 per game, as well as 10,525 rebounds, at 8.5 per game. He held numerous records in combined play stats for points, rebounds, assists, and steals. He was a two-time champion in the ABA, once in the NBA, and a Hall of Fame inductee in 1993.

RETIREMENT

After retirement, Erving became a businessman, showed his expertise as a television analyst, and had cameos in television programmes.

SUMMARY

As one of the most influential basketball players of all time, Julius Erving has been considered by many as one of the best dunkers ever. He helped the ABA to be seen as a worthwhile organization before the NBA era. In 1976, at an ABA slam dunk contest, he demonstrated a dunk from the free throw line. His move, the 'cradle dunk' has been cited as one of the best three plays in history. A Christian, Erving is the father of Alexandra Stevenson, a professional tennis player who reached the semi-finals of Wimbledon in 1999.

DAVID ROBINSON

Full Name	David Maurice Robinson
Nicknames	The Admiral
Main Position	Center
Nationality	American
NBA Debut	1989
Height	2.16m, or 7ft 1

CAREER

SAN ANTONIO SPURS
1989-2003

TROPHY CABINET

NBA Championship X2   Blocks Leader X1

(1998-99, 2002-03)   Season MVP X1

All-Star Game X10   Olympic Gold X2

Rookie of the Year X1

Scoring Leader X1

Rebounds Leader X1

All-NBA First Team X4

All-NBA Second Team X2

Defensive Player of the Year X1

All-Defensive First Team X4

All-Defensive Second Team X4

EARLY CAREER

David Maurice Robinson was born in the Key West area of Florida, USA. His father was in the US Navy. After settling in Virginia, he became proficient in school and most sports. Being only 5 foot 9 aged around 16 to 17, he achieved minimal basketball honors at high school.

Having graduated in 1983, he attended the US Naval academy, before eventually being drafted in 1987. However, because of navy commitments, Robinson did not compete in the NBA until 1989. He served as a junior lieutenant in the Navy. When he left the Navy, he was talked about as probably being the greatest player to have played at that level.

LATER CAREER

Robinson moved to the only team that he would play for in his career. After finishing the 1988/89 season with a disappointing 21 win, 61 loss result, the San Antonio Spurs improved to 56 wins, 26 losses the following season when Robinson joined the team. At the time, this was the greatest results turnaround in the NBA after one season. His impact led to the Rookie of the Year prize. The Spurs qualified for the playoffs and would participate in the latter stages for a few seasons more. He scored a franchise record 71 points against the Los Angeles Clippers in 1993/94, and with new signing Tim Duncan joining the line-up, the Spurs won their first NBA title in 1999. Robinson's partnership with Duncan became known as 'the twin towers'.

He suffered with back problems during his latter years, and in the final game of his career, he totalled 13 points and 17 rebounds, as San Antonio won game 6 of the 2003 Finals and the championship against the New Jersey Nets.

GREATEST ACHIEVEMENTS IN BASKETBALL

A two-time NBA and Olympic winner, Robinson excelled in the scoring, rebounds, and blocks stats, having accrued 20,790 points and 10,497 rebounds in over 980 games. A Hall of Fame was awarded in 2009, as well as receiving two Olympic HoF's. His admiral personality also led to the NBA Sportsmanship award in 2001, together with the Sports Illustrated' Sportsman of the Year 2003, and a Citizenship Award honour in 2003. His position was a 'center'.

RETIREMENT

After retiring, Robinson became a minority owner of his home team the San Antonio Spurs, and also was a co-owner of a car dealership. He was active in charity and philanthropic duties, and whilst in his playing days had a video game based on himself, produced by Sega.

SUMMARY

David Robinson has been mentioned as one of the best center players ever. Swift and mobile, he was also very adept at defence. His ball-handling skills were much admired. He had a potent midrange jumpshot, and was very effective in dunks and blocks. He supported and tutored Tim Duncan in his early days. His nickname came from his days in the Navy. Robinson has three sons.

DENNIS RODMAN

Full Name	Dennis Keith Rodman
Nicknames	The Worm, Dennis the Menace
Main Position	Power Forward
Nationality	American
NBA Debut	1986
Height	2.01m, or 6ft 7

CAREER

DETROIT PISTONS
1986-1993

SAN ANTONIO SPURS
1993-1995

CHICAGO BULLS
1995-1998

LOS ANGELES LAKERS
1998-1999

DALLAS MAVERICKS
1999-2000

TROPHY CABINET

NBA Championship   X5

(1988-89, 1989-90, 1995-96, 1996-97, 1997-98)

All Star Game   X2

Defensive Player of the Year   X2

Rebounds Leader   X7

All-Defensive First Team   X7

Al-Defensive Second Team   X1

Olympic Gold Medal   X2

EARLY CAREER

Born in the city of Trenton, New Jersey, in USA, Dennis Keith Rodman was attached to his mother at an early age. His father was in the Vietnam war. Both his sisters played basketball, but at a height of around 5 foot 6 at high school, he was left out of the football and basketball teams.

After leaving school he worked as a night janitor before he shot up to 6 foot 7, and achieved success at basketball in college. He managed to join the Detroit Pistons, a team labelled the 'bad boys' where he had many altercations with other players, and built up his reputation.

LATER CAREER

He soon matured into one of the best defensive players, as Detroit secured their second title in 1989/90. The 1991/2 season saw Rodman collect an amazing 18.7 rebounds per game and 1530 in total; still a record. One game in 1992, he gained 34 rebounds, a personal best.

After moving to San Antonio Spurs for the 1993/94 year, he decided to re-invent Mr. Rodman and put behind his 'shy imposter' image, starting to dye his hair different colours, and becoming more aggressive and confident in his approach to life. Headbutting referees and players, and getting involved in frequent clashes followed, before he won his seventh consecutive rebounding title in 1997/98.

The 1998 Finals saw Rodman win his fifth championship with some decisive play. In between the games though, he went off to take part in some professional wrestling. His NBA career ended in 2000, and after taking a long break from the game, Rodman played for some minor teams before finally retiring.

GREATEST ACHIEVEMENTS IN BASKETBALL

Rodman has the reputation of being one of the best defensive players ever, having accumulated 11,954 rebounds in 911 games, at an average of 13.1 per game. He only scored 6683 points, but won many defence and rebound awards in his career. He was a five-time NBA champion, and was inducted into the Hall of Fame in 2011. His main positions were 'small forward' and 'power forward'.

RETIREMENT

Rodman's personality has led him to star in films, take up professional wrestling, and participate in numerous reality shows. He was a regular for a while for the WCW wrestling promotion fighting mainly in tag team matches with Hulk Hogan. He also made frequent visits to North Korea taking part in basketball exhibitions. He has written several books, and had his own MTV talk show.

SUMMARY

Dennis Rodman has been touted as one of the best rebounding forwards to play in the NBA. He was a great defender, aggressive and fierce, and his rebounding abilities were some of the best seen on court. His outrageous personality off court has made him just as famous, with countless altercations, and an infamous short relationship with pop star Madonna.

HAKEEM OLAJUWON

Full Name	Hakeem Abdul Olajuwon
Nicknames	The Dream
Main Position	Center
Nationality	Nigerian, American
NBA Debut	1984
Height	2.13m, or 7ft 0

CAREER

HOUSTON ROCKETS
1984-2001

⬇

TORONTO RAPTORS
2001-2002

TROPHY CABINET

NBA Championship 🏆 X2   Season MVP 🏆 X1

(1993-94, 1994-95)   Finals MVP 🏆 X2

All-Star Game 🏆 X12   Blocks Leader 🏆 X3

Rebounds Leader 🏆 X2   Olympic Gold 🥇 X1

All-NBA First Team 🏆 X6

All-NBA Second Team 🏆 X3

All-Defensive First Team 🏆 X5

All-Defensive Second Team 🏆 X4

Defensive Player of the Year 🏆 X2

EARLY CAREER

Hakeem Abdul Olajuwon was born in the city of Lagos, Nigeria, in Africa. His parents owned a cement business. As a youth he was a soccer goalkeeper and struggled at basketball in school. It was when he emigrated to the USA and enrolled into the University of Houston in 1980 that Olajuwon started to excel in the sport, improving his game with the help of basketball MVP winner Moses Malone. It was during his time at college that he got his nickname 'the Dream' because of the way he was able to dunk the ball so effortlessly due to his great height.

LATER CAREER

Naturally, this led to a selection in the NBA draft of 1984. His first season with the Houston Rockets was characterized by the partnership with 7 foot 4 fellow teammate Ralph Sampson, known as the 'twin towers' duo. He quickly became a rebounds and blocked shot specialist in the following seasons, and in 1994 aided the Rockets to the NBA championship – the first professional sports title to come to Houston in 33 years. Olajuwon also became the first foreign-born player to win the MVP award. He showed some of his career-best form in the following season, outshining the likes of David Robinson and Shaquille O'Neal on the way to another title for the Rockets.

After moving to Toronto Raptors, Olajuwon achieved little success, and eventually, due to a back injury, retired in 2002. However, he left the game as the number one in blocked shots made in the history of the NBA.

GREATEST ACHIEVEMENTS
IN BASKETBALL

Olajuwon finished his career with an incredible 3830 blocks, the most in the history of the NBA, and 13,748 rebounds. He was a two-time NBA champion, MVP Finals winner, and the defensive, rebound, and blocks leader in many seasons. Added to his defensive prowess, he averaged 21.8 points per game, totalling 26,946 career points.

In 1238 career matches, he also averaged over 11 rebounds per game. He won the Olympic Gold with the USA team in 1996. He was inducted into the Hall of Fame in 2008. His main position was as a 'center'.

RETIREMENT

Olajuwon has prospered in the real estate market, and has a home in Jordan, in Asia. He has helped towards teaching younger players, and shown other soon-to-be established basketball stars some of his moves and playing style. Amongst them: Kobe Bryant and LeBron James. In 2006, a bronze monument was erected outside the Toyota Center, the home of the Houston Rockets, for whom he became one of their favourite icons and a much admired citizen.

SUMMARY

Hakeem Olajuwon has been considered as one of the greatest 'centers' in NBA history, and a potent clutch performer, performing well in pressure situations. His skill in defensive and offensive play was immense, and was especially praised for the way he stole the ball and blocked shots, particularly as he was a frontcourt player. Some commented on him having the best footwork ever seen on a big man in the league.

Full Name	Dwyane Tyrone Wade, Jr.
Nicknames	The Flash
Main Position	Shooting Guard
Nationality	American
NBA Debut	2003
Height	1.93m, or 6ft 4

CAREER

MIAMI HEAT
2003-2016

CLEVELAND CAVALIERS
2017-2018

CHICAGO BULLS
2016-2017

MIAMI HEAT
2018-2019

TROPHY CABINET

NBA Championship 🏆 X3

(2005-06, 2011-12, 2012-13)

All-Star Game 🏆 X13

Finals MVP 🏆 X1

Scoring Leader 🏆 X1

All-NBA First Team 🏆 X2

ALl-NBA Second Team 🏆 X3

All-Defensive Second Team 🏆 X3

Olympic Gold X1

EARLY CAREER

Dwyane Tyrone Wade Jr. was born in the city of Chicago, Illinois, and endured a difficult and challenging childhood. His mother took drugs and spent time in prison. He sought out the sports of basketball and football to avoid drugs and gangs. His idol at an early age was Michael Jordan. Wade was a superb wide receiver in football at high school. After a successful college basketball career, he was drafted as a pick for the NBA in 2003.

LATER CAREER

Playing for Miami Heat in 2006, Wade scored 42, 36, 43, and 36 points in consecutive matches, for an average of 34.7 points per game in his first finals, which gave his franchise the NBA title. He missed a succession of games in the 2006/07 season and needed surgery, before becoming the second player in NBA history to garner a stat of 40 points, 10 assists, and five blocks in one game two seasons later. Wade continued to rack up the scoring/assists numbers records in a host of games.

He eventually became Miami's all-time greatest points scorer, breaking records in the quadruple double (points/assists/steals/blocks) in matches along the way. His 10,000th career point came along in 2009/10, and he broke the franchise record of scoring 10 points or more in 148 consecutive games. LeBron James joined in 2010 and two more championships followed in succession. After trying out at two other clubs, Wade reunited with the Heat in 2018 accumulating more records in the statistical play figures. He retired in 2019. He was given the nickname 'flash' in reference to the song from the film 'Flash Gordon'.

GREATEST ACHIEVEMENTS IN BASKETBALL

In a 16-year career, Wade won three NBA titles, one MVP in Finals, and was Miami Heat's record holder in points, games, assists, and steals. He accumulated 23,165 career points in over a 1000 games, averaging 22 points a game. He also led the way when USA captured the Olympic Gold at the 2008 games. He was Sports Illustrated' Sportsman of the Year in 2006, and also named in the Time's 2020 list of the 100 most influential people. His position was a 'shooting guard'.

RETIREMENT

Wade took on a variety of ventures in retirement. He hosted the television show 'The Cube', had a line of endorsements, an executive position, and is involved in donating to charitable causes, including his own 'The Wade's World Foundation'.

SUMMARY

Dwyane Wade has four children and is a Christian. Being a shooting guard he was also able to play at point. He was very adept at driving close to the basket to score, doing so at great speed. He was also able to basket in difficult situations near the rim, even risking his body against much larger men. He has been featured in various publications and magazines as one of the best looking and best dressed men. The uncommon spelling of his first name (normally Dwayne), was given by his grandmother to his father, which he also inherited.

KOBE BRYANT

Full Name	Kobe Bean Bryant
Nicknames	Black Mamba
Main Position	Shooting Guard
Nationality	American
NBA Debut	1996
Height	1.98m, or 6ft 6

CAREER

LOS ANGELES LAKERS
1996-2016

TROPHY CABINET

NBA Championship 🏆 X5

(1990-00, 2000-01, 2001-02, 2008-09, 2009-10)

All-Star Game 🏆 X18

Season MVP 🏆 X1

Finals MVP 🏆 X2

Scoring Leader 🏆 X2

All-NBA First Team 🏆 X11

ALl-NBA Second Team 🏆 X2

All-Defensive First Team 🏆 X9

All-Defensive Second Team 🏆 X3

Olympic Gold 🥇 X2

EARLY CAREER

Born in Philadelphia, Pennsylvania, Kobe Bean Bryant is the son of former NBA player Joe Bryant. He started playing basketball at the age of three before the family moved to Italy, and continued to develop his game, taking an interest in association football at the same time. After moving back to the US, Bryant had a successful time at high school, and decided to go into the NBA without entering any colleges, at the age of only 17. In 1996 he signed a contract with the Los Angeles Lakers. He became the youngest Slam Dunk Contest winner in 1997, aged just 18, and after a slow start started to prosper, becoming one of the best shooting guards in the league.

LATER CAREER

In tandem with Shaquille O'Neal, Bryant helped the Lakers to win 67 games in the 1999/00 season, before winning the 2000 Finals, the franchise's first title since 1988. Bryant averaged 28.5 points in the 2000/01 season, including a 48 point and 16 rebound game in the playoffs. The next season he played 80 games and scored a career-best 56 points in one game, as the Lakers won their third successive championship. The 2002/03 season saw more records, with Bryant setting the mark for most three-pointers in a game, and then posting 40 points or more in nine successive matches.

After some troubling times, Bryant upped his game further during the 2005/06 season, with 62 points against the Dallas Mavericks in December 2005, and then a mammoth 81 points against the Toronto Raptors in January 2006, out of a team total of 122, second only to Wilt Chamberlain's 100-point record. He averaged 43.4 points for the month, and ended the season with 2832 points and 40 or more points in a game 27 times, both Lakers' records. More prolific high-scoring continued, with four straight games scoring 50 points or more in 2006/07. More championships followed in 2009 and 2010, collecting the youngest to 20,000 and 25,000 points along the way. Bryant naturally became the youngest to record 30,000 career points in December 2012, aged 34 years. Body pains, injuries, and surgery hampered his later years, but a return in 2014/15 saw him improve his numbers further. His final and record-breaking 20th season with the LA Lakers saw Bryant cheered at many venues, and finished his career with 60 points in his final game in April 2016.

GREATEST ACHIEVEMENTS IN BASKETBALL

In 1346 games in 20 years with the Los Angeles Lakers, Bryant scored 33,643 points, at 25 per game, recorded 7047 rebounds, and 6306 assists. He won the NBA championship five times, was two-time MVP in Finals, two-time scoring champion, won two Olympic Gold medalist, and was inducted into the Hall of Fame in 2020.

RETIREMENT

Bryant had many endorsements during and after his playing career, being one of the highest paid sportsman. He ventured into business, got involved in television and film work, and donated his time to charitable causes.

SUMMARY

Kobe Bryant has often been mentioned as one of the most dangerous scorers in NBA history. With comparisons to Michael Jordan, Bryant was a deft mover and a compulsive shooter, with a very high work ethic and commitment level. Bryant passed away tragically in January 2020, after a helicopter accident.

Full Name	Walter Ray Allen, Jr.
Nicknames	Mr. Basketball, Ray Ray
Main Position	Shooting Guard
Nationality	American
NBA Debut	1996
Height	1.96m, or 6ft 5

CAREER

MILWAUKEE BUCKS
1996-2003

BOSTON CELTICS
2007-2012

SEATTLE SUPERSONICS
2003-2007

MIAMI HEAT
2012-2014

TROPHY CABINET

NBA Championship X2

(2007-08, 2012-13)

All-Star Game  X10

All-NBA Second Team X1

All-NBA Third Team X1

Olympic Gold X1

EARLY CAREER

Walter Ray Allen Jr. was born at the Castle Air Force Base, near Merced, in California. He was a military child, living in Britain during that time, before settling in South Carolina where he attended high school. Due to this, he found it challenging dealing with other kids, but found solace in doing well in sports. A growth in height helped him to decide that basketball was his sport and, after a successful college career, was ready for the big time. He joined the Milwaukee Bucks in the 1996 draft.

LATER CAREER

After starting in all 82 games in the 1997/98 season, Allen signed the largest paid contract to date in 1999, excelling in the combined disciplines of points, rebounds, and assists. With three-point scoring coming more into the game, Allen moved into second place for three-point field goals in 2006, before breaking the record for the most three-pointers made in one season. He missed the rest of the 2006/07 season because of an ankle surgery.

Having joined the Boston Celtics in 2007, Allen was involved in the largest comeback victory in Finals history in June 2008, when he pocketed 19 points and nine rebounds against the Los Angeles Lakers. Five days later, he threw seven three-pointers in game 6 of the finals, as he claimed his inaugural NBA championship success. The next few seasons saw Allen continue his superb three-point making spree, culminating in him breaking the record for the most three-pointers in the NBA, with 2562, in February 2011. After sitting out a few seasons due to various issues, he decided to retire in 2016.

GREATEST ACHIEVEMENTS IN BASKETBALL

In a career spanning 1300 games, Allen attempted an amazing 7429 three-point field goal shots, and played 400 consecutive matches for the Bucks. He garnered 24,505 points at an average of 18.9 points per game, together with over 5200 rebounds and over 4300 assists. He also holds several three point and free throw records for both the Bucks and Celtics franchises. A two-time NBA winner, Allen also won an Olympic Gold, and was named the USA Basketball Male Athlete of the Year in 1995. His main position was as a 'shooting guard'.

RETIREMENT

Two years after retirement, Allen was inducted into the Hall of Fame. He starred in a few films, became an NBA spokesperson, and supported various charities. He had an autobiography written in 2018, and he worked as a head coach for a school in 2021. He also created the 'Ray of Hope' foundation to aid charitable work in various communities.

SUMMARY

Ray Allen once held the record for the most three-point shots made, an amazing statistic mainly dependant on his ability to make the jump shot with a straight and steady body, as well as a fluid, athletic movement on the court. He has four children, and has reported himself to have borderline OCD, to which he sees as an asset for his skilful and exceptional shooting style.

WILT CHAMBERLAIN

Full Name	Wilton Norman Chamberlain
Nicknames	The Big Dipper, Wilt the Stilt
Main Position	Center
Nationality	American
NBA Debut	1959
Height	2.16m, or 7ft 1

CAREER

PHILADELPHIA WARRIORS
1959-1962

PHILADELPHIA 76ERS
1964-1968

SAN FRANCISCO WARRIORS
1962-1964

LOS ANGELES LAKERS
1968-1973

TROPHY CABINET

NBA Championship X2
(1966-67, 1971-72)

Season MVP X4
Finals MVP X1

Scoring Leader X7
Assists Leader X1

Rebounds Leader X11

All-Star Game X13

All-NBA First Team X7

All-NBA Second Team X3

All-Defensive First Team X2

Rookie of the Year X1

EARLY CAREER

Wilton Norman Chamberlain was born in the largest city in the state of Pennsylvania, Philadelphia. He was a weak child, but grew up to be a keen track and field athlete before turning his attention to basketball. He was around 6 foot at the age of 10, and 6 foot 11 in high school. He soon became well known for his scoring and shot blocking abilities, and impressed with his prolific numbers, including 74, 78, and 90 points in three successive school games. He continued to show his all-round game in college, developing a variety of trademark shooting and general play.

Unable to join the NBA, Chamberlain played for the Harlem Globetrotters, including a historic visit to Moscow in 1959. He eventually made his debut for the Philadelphia Warriors as the highest paid NBA player. In his first game, he scored 43 points and had 28 rebounds.

LATER CAREER

The amazing numbers racked up and he finished his inaugural season averaging 37 points and 27 rebounds per game. Chamberlain also broke other records, and was not surprisingly the Rookie of the Year. He continued to break records in the scoring and rebounding charts, and became the only player to score over 4000 points in a season, in 1962, having attained the remarkable feat of 100 points in a game against the New York Knicks earlier in March. He shot 36 field goals and made 28 free throws in 48 minutes of playing time, reaching three figures with 46 seconds to go.

After moving to the Philadelphia 76ers, Chamberlain finally won the NBA championship in 1967, notching 41 rebounds in one game during the Finals. The next season, he was the league leader with 702 assists, before becoming the first player in history to reach 25,000 career points. A fight with boxing great Muhammad Ali was talked about in 1971, but never took place. A move to Los Angeles Lakers saw Chamberlain win his second crown after being named the captain, having suffered at the finals stage in previous years. The 1973 Finals turned out to be the last few games of his career, ending in style with a dunk.

GREATEST ACHIEVEMENTS IN BASKETBALL

Chamberlain was the holder of several scoring records at the time of his retirement, as well as a superb rebounding record. In 1045 games, he scored 31,419 points at an average of 30.1 points a game, and 23,924 rebounds, at 22.9 a game. He was twice NBA champion, four times MVP, scoring and rebounding champion on numerous occasions, and inducted into the Hall of Fame in 1979. His position was as a 'center'.

RETIREMENT

Soon after retiring, Chamberlain coached an ABA team, before going into business ventures and the entertainment industry. He starred with Arnold Schwarzenegger in the 1984 film, Conan the Destroyer.

SUMMARY

Wilt Chamberlain will go down in history as one of the most dominant scorers in basketball history. He was also a fantastic rebounding player, holding a multitude of records in both categories. He never married, and passed away in 1999 due to heart failure.

SCOTTIE PIPPEN

Full Name	Scotty Maurice Pippen Sr.
Nicknames	No Tippin' Pippen, Batman
Main Position	Small Forward
Nationality	American
NBA Debut	1987
Height	2.03m, or 6ft 8

CAREER

CHICAGO BULLS
1987-1998

PORTLAND TRAIL BLAZERS
1999-2003

HOUSTON ROCKETS
1998-1999

CHICAGO BULLS
2003-2004

TROPHY CABINET

NBA Championship   X6

(90-91, 91-92, 92-93, 95-96, 96-97, 97-98)

All-Star Game   X7

Steals Leader   X1

All-NBA First Team   X3

All-NBA Second Team   X2

All-Defensive First Team   X8

All-Defensive Second Team   X2

Olympic Gold X2

EARLY CAREER

Born in the city of Hamburg, Arkansas, Scotty Maurice Pippen Sr. was the youngest of 12 children. Both his parents were over 6 feet tall. Pippen played point guard at high school, and was only 6 foot 1 when he graduated. When he became a part of the Chicago Bulls team, he formed a young forward duo with Horace Grant, who was 6 feet 10. His teammate and mentor in those early days was Michael Jordan.

LATER CAREER

Pippen developed the main role of a defensive stop when the Bulls acquired their three titles between 1991 and 1993. His scoring and all-round play benefitted due to the guidance from Jordan. After Jordan retired in 1993, Pippen took on the mantle of the leader and ended the 1994/95 season as the club's number one in points, rebounds, assists, steals and blocks. With the return of Jordan and the addition of Dennis Rodman, Pippen would go on to win his fourth title with the Bulls. Later on, he would go on to receive the player of the week accolade for the fifth and last time.

When he joined the Houston Rockets in 1998, Pippen made the solo cover of premier sports magazine, Sports Illustrated. However, he departed after one year partly due to conflicts on court with some of his teammates. He played all 82 games in his first season with the Portland Trail Blazers, before returning to the Chicago Bulls aged 37. Inflicted by injuries, Pippen played his final career game in February 2004, on the court for only eight minutes. This was the only time he had failed to make the playoffs, having participated in them in his previous 16 seasons. A return to competitive play saw him compete in Finland and Sweden in 2008, aged 42.

GREATEST ACHIEVEMENTS IN BASKETBALL

In 17 seasons, Pippen won six NBA championships, appeared in numerous All-Star and All-NBA teams, won two Olympic titles, and finished with a total of 18,940 points, 7494 rebounds, and 6135 assists. He was one of the few players to achieve a total of 200 steals and 100 blocks in a season, and attained nearly 1000 three-point scores. His main position was as a 'small forward'.

RETIREMENT

Pippen tried his hand at being an executive with the Chicago Bulls, and had a bronze statue unveiled in 2011, located inside the Bulls' home arena, the United Center in Chicago. He has also appeared on television many times, and the Hall of Fame accolade was given to him in 2010.

SUMMARY

Scottie Pippen has always been held in high regard for his defensive abilities. Seen as an expert at that role, Pippen used his long arms to good effect, and with a determined work ethic, was a team player with countless assists made. He struggled with jumping to shoot early on in his career, but his legacy has seen him make a series of 'all-time' lists. One unfortunate reputation he had was for being a poor 'tipper' at restaurants!

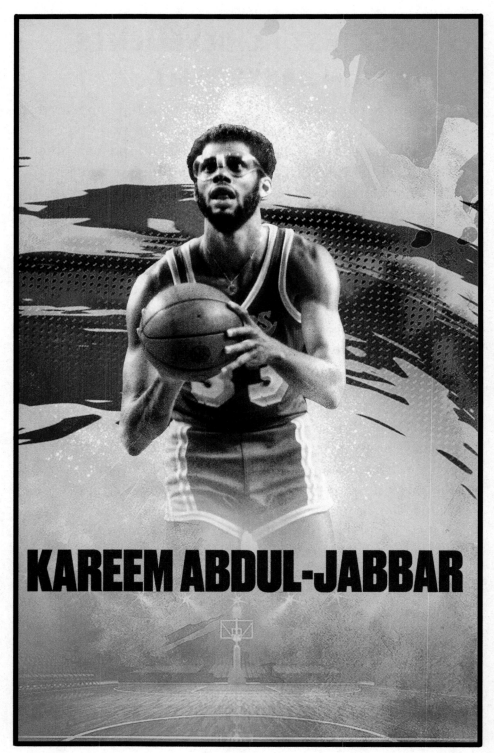

KAREEM ABDUL-JABBAR

Full Name	Ferdinand Lewis Alcindor Jr.
Nicknames	Lew, Cap
Main Position	Center
Nationality	American
NBA Debut	1969
Height	2.18m, or 7ft 2

CAREER

MILWAUKEE BUCKS
1969-1975

→

LOS ANGELES LAKERS
1975-1989

TROPHY CABINET

NBA Championship 🏆 X6

(70-71, 79-80, 81-82, 84-85, 86-87, 87-88)

All-Star Game 🏆 X19   Season MVP 🏆 X6

Rebounds Leader 🏆 X1   Finals MVP 🏆 X2

Blocks Leader 🏆 X4

All-NBA First Team 🏆 X10

All-NBA Second Team 🏆 X5

All-Defensive First Team 🏆 X5

All Defensive Second Team 🏆 X6

Rookie of the Year 🏆 X1

Scoring Leader 🏆 X2

EARLY CAREER

Ferdinand Lewis Alcindor Jr. was born in the district of Harlem, New York, USA. He weighed a staggering 12 pounds 11 at birth, and by the age of nine was already 5 foot 8 tall. He has no brothers or sisters. His rapid growth spurt continued to 6 foot 8 when he was 13 to 14 years old, and he was able to slam dunk a basket easily.

He produced a record 2067 points for his NYC high school, and competing as a lowly freshman helped his side to beat a strong varsity team. An incredible 56 points followed in his first Varsity game in 1966, despite the authorities going on to ban the 'dunk' shot because of his dominance in the game! Alcindor converted to Islam in 1968, eventually changing his name (though not using it in public for another three years), and qualified with a Bachelor of Arts degree in 1969. It was at this time that he took up martial arts.

LATER CAREER

Abdul-Jabbar turned down the lucrative chance to play for the Harlem Globetrotters, and instead joined the Milwaukee Bucks in 1969, gaining the Rookie of the Year award. Two years later, the Bucks won the NBA title, with Abdul-Jabbar aged only 24. He perfected his trademark 'skyhook' shot, using a sweeping high arm and his reach to shoot over the defender. He went to the Los Angeles Lakers in 1975 and stayed there for his last 14 seasons, winning five NBA titles in the process.

He also started to wear goggles on court to prevent further eye damage having had his cornea scratched on a few occasions. In 1984, Abdul-Jabbar broke Wilt Chamberlain's record for the most points by an individual player in NBA history. When he called it a day in 1989, aged 42, Abdul-Jabbar held a plethora of records, some of which still stand today.

GREATEST ACHIEVEMENTS IN BASKETBALL

In a distinguished career, Abdul-Jabbar played in 20 seasons of the NBA, being on the winning side six times, and two MVPs in Finals, as well as gaining six MVP's, and representing All-Star teams, both of which were records at the time. During his tenure, he participated in the playoffs 18 times, and reached the finals ten times. His total of 38,387 points (average of 24.6 per game), and his career wins (1074), still stand today as records in the NBA. Other records he held at the time were games played, field goals, blocked shots, and minutes played. He was Rookie of the year in 1970, and inducted into the Hall of Fame in 1995. His one position was as a 'center'.

RETIREMENT

Abdul-Jabbar has written a book, and became a basketball coach, having twice tried the role as an assistant. He received the Presidential Medal of Freedom in 2016 from the then president Barack Obama.

SUMMARY

Karim Abdul-Jabbar has been called by some as the greatest basketball player of all time, according to his numbers, with some placing him second behind Michael Jordan. He trained as a martial artist and appeared in the film 'Game of Death' in 1978, where he had a lengthy fight scene with Bruce Lee. Lee actually tutored Abdul-Jabbar in the style of martial art fighting.

KARL MALONE

Full Name	Karl Anthony Malone
Nicknames	The Mailman
Main Position	Power Forward
Nationality	American
NBA Debut	1985
Height	2.06m, or 6ft 9

CAREER

UTAH JAZZ
1985-2003

LOS ANGELES LAKERS
2003-2004

TROPHY CABINET

All-Star Game X14

Season MVP X2

All-NBA First Team  X11

All-NBA Second Team X2

All-Defensive First Team X3

All-Defensive Second Team X1

Olympic Gold X2

EARLY CAREER

Karl Anthony Malone was born in the community of Summerfield, Louisiana, USA, and lived on a farm with his single mother and eight siblings. Despite working on the farm, fishing and chopping trees, he gained a succession of titles at his high school. He attended Louisiana Tech University and played college basketball.

When the 1985 NBA draft came around, Malone was actually the 13th pick overall, which is mentioned in his NBA biography, wondering why he was picked so low considering the impact he was to have on the game in the future.

LATER CAREER

Malone joined the Utah Jazz in 1985, and by the second season was one of the leading scorers in the NBA. He formed a great partnership with John Stockton, a point guard specialist, and in the 1988 playoffs scored 31 points in the seventh game against the eventual champions, the Los Angeles Lakers. His average went up to a fantastic 31 points and 11 rebounds per game in the 1989/90 season, and during a game in 1990 scored a massive 61 points, having pocketed 52 in a game, a month earlier.

Early in 1991, he top scored in a remarkable 19 consecutive games for the Jazz. This was followed by two Olympic Golds in 1992 & 1996. The first two NBA Finals of his career ended in disappointment, losing both times to the Chicago Bulls in 1997 and 1998. Malone competed in one season for the LA Lakers in 2003/04, and despite missing most of the season due to injury, his team reached the final before losing to the Detroit Pistons. He eventually retired in 2005.

GREATEST ACHIEVEMENTS IN BASKETBALL

Despite not winning the NBA title with any team, he won the MVP twice, appeared in numerous All-Star games, and participated in every playoffs during his career. The total of 36,928 points in 1476 matches put him in second place for the highest points scorer in the NBA, averaging 25 points per game. He also holds numerous free throws records in baskets made and attempted. He was inducted into the Hall of Fame in 2010. He developed the nickname 'the Mailman' due to ability to 'deliver', and his accurate and efficient scoring in the post position. His main playing position was the 'power forward'.

RETIREMENT

Malone had a bronze statue of himself put outside the Utah Jazz arena. He made donations to politics, is a keen fisherman, business owner, appeared on tv shows, and in 1998 participated in a professional wrestling match. Starring in the WCW promotion he fought in a tag team match against fellow basketball star Dennis Rodman and Hulk Hogan.

SUMMARY

Apart from his record-breaking scoring, Malone was a free throw specialist, having attained the free throws record by the end of his career. His defending and rebounding was done with great physical ability, and he maintained this standard even into his 40s. His presence enabled him to beat most forwards to the ball, and he was able to run the play on court proficiently.

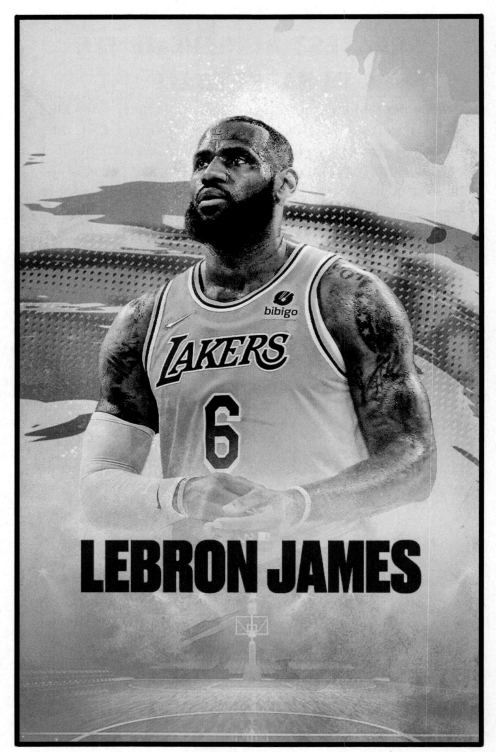

Full Name	LeBron Raymone James
Nicknames	King James
Main Position	Small Forward / Power Forward
Nationality	American
NBA Debut	2003
Height	2.06m, or 6ft 9

CAREER

CLEVELAND CAVALIERS
2003-2010

CLEVELAND CAVALIERS
2014-2018

MIAMI HEAT
2010-2014

LOS ANGELES LAKERS
2018-2022 (STILL ACTIVE)

TROPHY CABINET

NBA Championship 🏆 X4

(2011-12, 2012-13, 2015-16, 2019-20)

All-Star Game 🏆 X18   Season MVP 🏆 X4

Scoring Leader 🏆 X1   Finals MVP 🏆 X4

Assists Leader 🏆 X1   Olympic Gold 🥇 X2

All-NBA First Team 🏆 X13

All-NBA Second Team 🏆 X3

ALl-Defensive First Team 🏆 X5

All Defensive Second Team 🏆 X1

Rookie of the Year 🏆 X1

EARLY CAREER

LeBron Raymone James Sr. was born in the city of Akron, in Ohio, USA. His mother was only 16 at the time of his birth and life was a struggle due to an absent father. After moving in with a local football coach, James started playing basketball and competed in an amateur league.

Due to some success, James then decided to attend a private Catholic high school. More outstanding play followed which duly led to an NBA draft interest, and he was also a natural at American football. James was picked by the Cleveland Cavaliers for the 2003/04 season and in his very first game picked up 25 points, a new record for a debutant. More stellar performances helped him to pick up the Rookie of the Year award.

LATER CAREER

A game in 2005 saw James accumulate 56 points, a new club record, and he helped the Cavaliers to reach the playoffs the following year. However, after a disappointing loss in an end-of-season game in 2010, he became an available free agent.

Despite heavy criticism from all corners, he joined up with Miami Heat, a team that became seen as a side of 'villians'. Undeterred, James helped them to the 2011 Finals, before winning the championship the following season. His playoff run saw him average just over 30 points a game. His dominance grew and in 2013 he became the youngest player to reach 20,000 points in the NBA. This led to another title, aided by a 27-game winning streak during the league season. He achieved another goal scoring record in March 2014, with 61 points in one game.

He re-joined the Cleveland Cavaliers in 2014, this time as a hero, and helped the city to win its first title in professional sports for 52 years, when Cleveland came back from 3-1 down to win the 2016 final, 4-3! This was his sixth successive NBA Finals appearance. He extended this to eight in 2018. His success continues, with the 2020 title going to his present team, the Los Angeles Lakers.

GREATEST ACHIEVEMENTS IN BASKETBALL

With his career still ongoing, James has still more accolades to add to his CV. He recently became the first man to score 10 points or more in a 1000 consecutive games, and the youngest to reach 35,000 points in the NBA. He has so far won two Olympic gold medals, and, as of date, played in over 1300 games averaging around 27 points per game. Four NBA titles (three different franchises), ten finals, four MVPs in Finals, All-star rookie, and scoring leader, are just some of the career highlights to date. His main position is as a 'Small Forward' & 'Power Forward'.

SUMMARY

LeBron James has been compared with the great Michael Jordan, and apart from being an immense offensive player, has developed into a strong defensive player, using his height and athletic ability in all areas of the court. He has numerous endorsement contracts, is currently the highest paid basketball player, active in charity work, and has a part ownership of Liverpool FC. He followed Jordan by appearing in the 2021 film, 'Space Jam: A New Legacy'.

PAUL PIERCE

Full Name	Paul Anthony Pierce
Nicknames	The Truth
Main Position	Small Forward
Nationality	American
NBA Debut	1999
Height	1.98m, or 6ft 6

CAREER

BOSTON CELTICS
1998-2013

WASHINGTON WIZARDS
2014-2015

BROOKLYN NETS
2013-2014

LOS ANGELES CLIPPERS
2015-2017

TROPHY CABINET

NBA Championship (2007-08) — X1

All-Star Game — X10

Finals MVP — X1

All-NBA Second Team — X1

All-NBA Third Team — X3

EARLY CAREER

Paul Anthony Pierce was born and raised in Oakland, California, USA. After a difficult start, Pierce prospered during his college career, and grew up supporting the Los Angeles Lakers. He spent three years at the Kansas Jayhawks college team before entering the 1998 draft. Pierce was picked by the Boston Celtics, a team he did not like growing up. In the 2000/01 season, he played all 82 games averaging 25 points per game.

LATER CAREER

Pierce helped the Celtics to reach the playoffs for the first time in seven years in 2002. Playing the New Jersey Nets in one of the games, they overturned a record 21 point deficit to win, with Pierce scoring 28 points. He top-scored in 2001/02 with 2144 points. The addition of Ray Allen and Kevin Garnett in the 2007/08 season helped the Celtics to win 66 matches during the regular season, having only won 24 the previous year. They reached the 2008 Finals, where Pierce took the MVP and averaged nearly 22 points per game in the 4-2 victory over the Los Angeles Lakers.

He won the three-point contest in 2010, before reaching two milestones playing for Boston; his 20,000th point in a Celtics shirt in 2010, and 1000 career games in 2012. Disappointment followed in several playoffs, despite Pierce performing brilliantly in individual play. He played 75 games for his new team the Brooklyn Nets in 2013/14, collecting another 1000 points for the 15th season in a row. He spent just one season at the Nets, deciding to move to Washington Wizards, where he also spent just one term. A 2000th career three-pointer duly followed to add to his other numerous records. When he retired in 2017, he signed a non-playing contract with the Boston Celtics so that he could officially retire with that team.

GREATEST ACHIEVEMENTS IN BASKETBALL

Pierce competed in 1343 games, and was both an NBA champion and MVP Finals winner in 2008. He appeared on several All-Star teams, and holds many Boston Celtics franchise records, mainly in free throws. He scored 26,397 career points (average 19.7 per game), had 7527 rebounds, and 4708 assists. His position was a 'small forward'.

RETIREMENT

Pierce worked as a broadcast analyst on ESPN, and helped towards funding the hospital that treated him when he was severely injured. He founded 'The Truth Fund' which does charitable work to help children, and for which he received an NBA Community Service award.

SUMMARY

With his strength and athletic ability, Paul Pierce has been considered as one of the best shooters of all-time. Pierce also represented the USA in the World Championships, and will always be remembered for having a superb all-round game, achieving high numbers in the stats plays. He got his nickname from fellow basketball star Shaquille O'Neal who mentioned the word after an awesome performance against him in a game in 2001, when Pierce scored 42 points. He has three children.

Full Name	Vincent Lamar Carter Jr.
Nicknames	Vinsanity
Main Position	Shooting Guard
Nationality	American
NBA Debut	1999
Height	1.98m, or 6ft 6

CAREER

TORONTO RAPTORS
1998-2004

DALLAS MAVERICKS
2011-2014

NEW JERSEY NETS
2004-2009

MEMPHIS GRIZZLIES
2014-2017

ORLANDO MAGIC
2009-2010

SACRAMENTO KINGS
2017-2018

PHOENIX SUNS
2010-2011

ATLANTA HAWKS
2018-2020

TROPHY CABINET

All-Star Game　　　　X8

All-NBA Second Team　　X1

All-NBA Third Team　　X1

Rookie of the Year　　X1

Olympic Gold　　X1

EARLY CAREER

Born in sunny Daytona Beach, Florida, Vincent Lamar Carter Jr. played football at high school as a quarterback, and volleyball. Success at college led to a place on the Toronto Raptors team in 1998. Some spectacular dunks saw him pick up the nickname 'Air Canada' and the Rookie of the Year award. A first ever playoff appearance for the franchise followed in 2000.

LATER CAREER

Carter displayed an amazing assortment of dunks at the 2000 All-Star weekend, but from 2001 started suffering with knee and hamstring problems. During a game in December 2001, he produced a career-high quadruple double of 42 points, 15 rebounds, six assists, and five steals, one of the best ever all-round performances in the NBA. A surgery, followed by a tumultuous move to New Jersey Nets, saw Carter booed on his return to the Toronto arena in 2005. He had left the Raptors after scoring 9420 points in six-and-a-half years there.

In December 2005, he created an NBA record by executing the most free throws in one quarter, with 16. His five years at the Nets saw him average 23.6 points per game, as the franchise reached three playoffs in succession. After moving to Orlando Magic, he participated in the only Conference finals of his career in 2010. He reached the milestone of 20,000 points in 2011, and 1500 three-pointers in 2012. He secured many records past the age of 40, including the 25,000 point mark in 2018, the oldest player to score 20 points or more in a game aged 41, and the only player to play in four different decades. In January 2020, he reached third spot in the most appearances by an individual player, and retirement followed in June.

GREATEST ACHIEVEMENTS IN BASKETBALL

Carter played in 22 seasons, the most by an NBA player, and for eight different franchises. He won an Olympic gold in 2000, was the slam dunk champ in the same year, the teammate of the year in 2016, and he received the NBA Sportsmanship award in 2020. In 1541 games, Carter scored 25,728 points, at an average of 16.7 per game. His main position was as a 'shooting guard' and 'small forward'.

RETIREMENT

Carter is now a basketball analyst with ESPN, having opened a restaurant, and appeared in a film. He established the 'Embassy of Hope Foundation' and in 2000 was the child advocate of the year, before being awarded the Florida Governor's Points of Light award in 2007 for the philanthropic work in his home state.

SUMMARY

Vince Carter has been considered by some as the most talented player ever with his amazing leaping ability and a vast array of spectacular slam dunks. He was mainly a shooting guard and small forward, but also played as a power forward later in his career. He was also a prolific three-point scorer in his career.

KEVIN DURANT

Full Name	Kevin Wayne Durant
Nicknames	KD, Durantula
Main Position	Small Forward
Nationality	American
NBA Debut	2007
Height	2.08m, or 6ft 10

CAREER

SEATTLE SUPERSONICS
2007-2008

GOLDEN STATE WARRIORS
2016-2019

OKLAHOMA CITY THUNDER
2008-2016

BROOKLYN NETS
2019-2022 (STILL ACTIVE)

TROPHY CABINET

NBA Championship X2

(2016-17, 2017-18)

Season MVP X1

Olympic Gold X3

All-Star Game X12

Rookie of the Year X1

Finals MVP X2

Scoring Leader X4

ALl-NBA First Team X6

All-NBA Second Team X3

EARLY CAREER

Kevin Wayne Durant was born in the capital of the USA, Washington DC. He was 6 feet tall at the age of 13 to 14, and wanted to play basketball for his favourite team, the Toronto Raptors.

He became the first freshman to win the national college player of the year award, and duly declared his interest to join the NBA in 2007. He was signed up by the Seattle SuperSonics aged just 19 years, and managed 20 points per game in his first season, to secure the Rookie of the Year prize. The following year, the SuperSonics changed location and renamed themselves the Oklahoma City Thunder.

LATER CAREER

The 2009/10 season saw Durant become the youngest NBA scoring champion with an average of 30 points a game, and with figures of 27.7 and 28, also won the accolade in the next two seasons. He was also the youngest to join the 50-40-90 club in 2012/13, a high percentage rate on field goal shooting, three-point shooting, and free throw shooting made in a season. The prodigious scoring continued, and in 2013/14 he chalked up 30 points or more for 12 games in succession, before breaking Michael Jordan's record of 25 points or more in 41 successive matches.

Injury problems hampered him the next season, before eventually deciding to join up with the Golden State Warriors in 2016, the team that had defeated Oklahoma in the Conference finals the previous season. The Warriors won the championship in 2017, with Durant picking up yet another 'youngest' record; this time in reaching 20,000 points. He missed the 2019/20 season, having signed for the

Brooklyn Nets, before making his first team debut in December 2020. In an amazing run, Durant scored 39, 42, 49, and 48 points during a series of games in the 2021 playoffs. He is currently still with the Nets.

GREATEST ACHIEVEMENTS IN BASKETBALL

With a career still ongoing, Durant has so far won two NBA titles, two MVP in Finals, four scoring titles, three Olympic gold medals, and the 2010 World Championship with the USA team. So far he has averaged 27 points per game in his career, and has been named USA basketball male athlete of the year three times. His main position is 'small forward'.

SUMMARY

Kevin Durant has been widely considered as one of the best players of his generation, some say the best in the NBA at the moment, and others as one of the best of all time. As a small forward, he is very potent near the rim, having been an isolation player early on in his career. He is one of the most popular players on the circuit. Outside of basketball, Durant is well known for his philanthropy, has opened a restaurant, presented a YouTube channel, and in 2018 was named in the Time magazine, as one of the 100 most influential people.

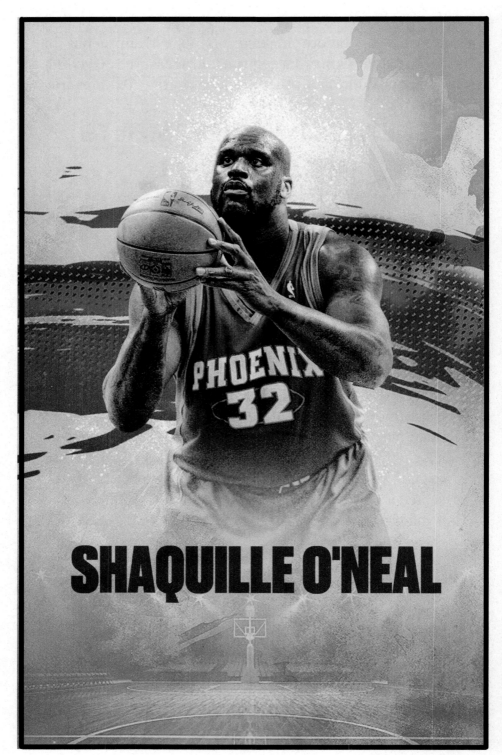

SHAQUILLE O'NEAL

Full Name	Shaquille Rashaun O'Neal
Nicknames	Shaq, The Diesel
Main Position	Center
Nationality	American
NBA Debut	1992
Height	2.16m, or 7ft 1

CAREER

ORLANDO MAGIC
1992-1996

MIAMI HEAT
2004-2007

CLEVELAND CAVALIERS
2009-2010

LOS ANGELES LAKERS
1996-2004

PHOENIX SUNS
2007-2009

BOSTON CELTICS
2010-2011

TROPHY CABINET

NBA Championship 🏆 X4

(1999-00, 2000-01, 2001-02, 2005-06)

All-Star Game 🏆 X15   Season MVP 🏆 X1

Scoring Leader 🏆 X2   Finals MVP 🏆 X3

Rookie of the Year 🏆 X1   Olympic Gold 🥇 X1

All-NBA First Team 🏆 X8

All-NBA Second Team 🏆 X2

All-Defensive Second Team 🏆 X3

EARLY CAREER

Shaquille Rashaun O'Neal was born in the city of Newark, New Jersey, USA, and grew up in difficult circumstances. He was 6 foot 6 by the age of 13, and after living for a while in Germany, he moved to Texas, USA.

With a height of 6 foot 10, O'Neal started playing basketball at high school at the age of 16. He impressed with his own 'hook shots' and studied at University before deciding to become an NBA player. He was picked by Orlando Magic in 1992, and duly took the player of the week award in his first week there. A string of good performances saw him secure the Rookie of the Year award.

LATER CAREER

O'Neal improved with his all-round game averaging 29.3 points per game in 1994/95, and 28 in his first finals appearance. A move to Los Angeles Lakers saw him help his team to three consecutive titles in the eight seasons he was there. O'Neal scored 61 points during a game in 2000, and was MVP in the finals all three times that the Lakers won the title from 2000 to 2002. During that time, injuries and on-field confrontations became the norm. A troublesome toe injury required surgery. Tensions and conflicts with the Lakers saw O'Neal make a move to Miami Heat in 2004.

His presence in the first season helped Miami Heat to win 59 matches, and a place in the playoffs. More injuries followed, but the high scoring continued, which eventually led to a title in 2006. After a dip in scoring, he experienced a resurgence after moving to the Phoenix Suns. He produced a 45-point and 11 rebound game in 2009. Further moves to the Cleveland Cavaliers and Boston Celtics made the aging

O'Neal realise that time was catching up with him, and needing regular medical treatment, he eventually announced his retirement in 2011.

GREATEST ACHIEVEMENTS IN BASKETBALL

In a long career spanning 1207 games, O'Neal scored 28,596 points, at an average of 23.7 points per game, and secured 13,099 rebounds, at 10.9 per game. Four-times with the champion team, three-time MVP in Finals, several All-Star games, and twice scoring champion, were achieved on top of an Olympic Gold medal and a Hall of Fame honor in 2016. He also won an award for a cable television programme he was involved with during his playing days. His position was as a 'center'.

RETIREMENT

O'Neal has been just as active off court, as when he was on it, with a succession of ventures, including rap albums, starring in films, his own tv shows, business dealings, mixed martial arts, and appearances in several commercials. He has also had brief stints in professional wrestling, guest starring for a variety of promotions, including taking part in a battle royal match. He is currently a basketball analyst for the NBA on television.

SUMMARY

Shaquille O'Neal became famous for his large stature and substantial presence on court. He overpowered many opponents with his physical strength and had the ability to dunk and shoot with accuracy. He was also an effective defender.

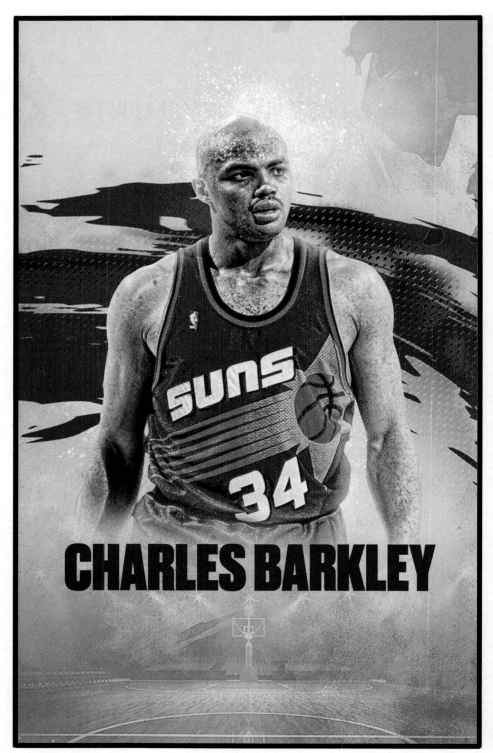

CHARLES BARKLEY

Full Name	Charles Wade Barkley
Nicknames	Sir Charles, Chuck
Main Position	Power Forward
Nationality	American
NBA Debut	1984
Height	1.98m, or 6ft 6

CAREER

PHILADELPHIA 76ERS
1984-1992

PHOENIX SUNS
1992-1996

HOUSTON ROCKETS
1996-2000

TROPHY CABINET

All-Star Game X11

Season MVP X1

Rebounds Leader X1

All-NBA First Team X5

All-NBA Second Team X5

Olympic Gold X2

EARLY CAREER

Charles Wade Barkley was born and raised in the small suburb of Leeds, Alabama, USA. His parents divorced when he was young. As a 5 foot 10 junior, he eventually became a popular player at college with his aptitude at dunks and blocks in spite of his short height and large frame. He played center and received many awards.

He was picked by the Philadelphia 76ers in 1984, joining a host of legends who had already helped the team to win the championship the previous year.

LATER CAREER

Mentored by Moses Malone, Barkley adapted to the playing style that was needed in that division, controlling his weight and preparing for games. He praised Malone for being the most influential person in his basketball career. During the 1987/88 season, he starred in 80 games and ended up with an average of 28.3 points and 11.9 rebounds per game. With the established players either leaving or retiring, Barkley quickly became the franchise lead player, and even made it onto the front cover of Sports Illustrated. In 1989/90 he was named Player of the Year by two publications. The 1991/92 season was his final year with the 76ers. His eight seasons with Philadelphia had made him into a household name, and he was top scorer for the franchise for six successive seasons.

In his first season with the Phoenix Suns he won the Most Valuable Player award, but from 1993/94 he was troubled by back pains. Further injury problems plagued him for the next few seasons, and when he retired he was, at the time, only the second player to have combined the playing stat of 23,000 points, 12,000 rebounds, and 4000 assists throughout his career.

GREATEST ACHIEVEMENTS IN BASKETBALL

In 16 seasons and with three teams, Barkley played 1073 games, and had an average of 22.1 points per game (total 23,757 points), and 11.7 rebounds per game (total 12,546). One MVP, a rebound leader, two Olympic Golds, and a Hall of Fame in 2006, were the other accolades he received. His position has been as a 'power forward'.

RETIREMENT

Barkley has become just as well known off the court as when he was on it. He is a regular television analyst, has written books, been in a film, shown interest in politics, and featured in numerous video games. His outspoken views have also generated much interest.

SUMMARY

Charles Barkley played mainly in the power forward position, but also tried his hand in the center and small forward positions. Despite his stocky physique and short stature, he was a potent rebounder and accurate shooter, capable of scoring points from anywhere on the court. He is popular with the fans and the media, and was well known for his on-field confrontations with fellow players and the crowd in attendance, leading to much controversy. Barkley has always been an advocate of the fact that sportspeople/athletes should not be seen as role models, not even himself.

Full Name	Larry Joe Bird
Nicknames	Larry Legend
Main Position	Forward
Nationality	American
NBA Debut	1979
Height	2.06m, or 6ft 9

CAREER

BOSTON CELTICS
1979-1992

TROPHY CABINET

NBA Championship   X3

(1980-81, 1983-84, 1985-86)

All-Star Game   X12

Season MVP   X3

Finals MVP   X2

All-NBA First Team   X9

All-NBA Second Team   X1

All-Defensive Second Team   X3

Rookie of the Year   X1

Olympic Gold   X1

EARLY CAREER

Born in the small town of West Baden Springs, Indiana, USA, Larry Joe Bird was brought up in the nearby town of French Lick. His father was a Korean War veteran. He came from a poor background and there were family problems, which led to him playing basketball for his high school. He averaged an amazing 31 points per game, which duly led to a scholarship in college basketball in 1974, but due to the difference in lifestyle, dropped out. He worked before attending university in 1975, and graduated with a Bachelor of Science degree in physical education in 1979. His college career was glittered with awards and honours.

LATER CAREER

Bird started his pro career at the Boston Celtics in 1979, and was soon awarded a $3.25 million contract, the highest paid for a rookie player. He made an immediate impact in his first season playing all 82 games, impressing in all combined play numbers, and picking up the Rookie of the Year award. Aided by the trio of Bird, Kevin McHale, and Robert Parish, the Celtics won the 1981 title, and some staggering numbers in points, rebounds, and assists, saw Bird elevated to great heights. A record 60 points followed against the Atlanta Hawks in 1985.

However, back problems started to occur, which would trouble him for the rest of his career, but undeterred Bird put in a tremendous 29 points, 11 rebounds, and 12 assists in game 6 of the 1986 Finals, as Boston lifted the NBA crown. Many have considered this Celtics side to be the number one team in NBA history. Bird was also in direct competition with Magic Johnson throughout the 80s, in the era of the Lakers-Celtics showdowns. Magic won five titles, Bird three, during this time. Continuing back problems meant Bird had to hang up his boots in 1992.

GREATEST ACHIEVEMENTS IN BASKETBALL

To go with his three NBA championships, Bird was the Most Valuable Player in the Finals two times, an Olympic Gold medal winner, and during his career averaged a brilliant 24.3 points, 10 rebounds, and 6.3 assists per game played. He added a superb 1556 steals to his statistics. He has been named as both the executive and coach of the year in the NBA. He was a 'small forward' and 'power forward'.

RETIREMENT

Bird was inducted into the Hall of Fame twice, the first in 1998. He took up coaching and executive positions, starred in movies, appeared in video games, and a song was written after him. He also wrote a book with Magic Johnson, with whom he had a great rivalry in the 1980s. Despite their many battles on court, they remained great friends. In 2019, Bird was awarded with the NBA Lifetime Achievement Award, which he shared with Johnson.

SUMMARY

Larry Bird played in both the small forward and power forward positions, and was seen as one of the best shooters of all time. He was a superb pressure player, a 'clutch' and an efficient passer of the ball and defender in spite of being a slow mover. Bird himself said that he practiced three-point shots with his eyes closed.

TIM DUNCAN

Full Name	Timothy Theodore Duncan
Nicknames	The Big Fundamental
Main Position	Power Forward / Center
Nationality	U.S Virgin Islands, American
NBA Debut	1997
Height	2.11m, or 6ft 11

CAREER

SAN ANTONIO SPURS
1997-2016

TROPHY CABINET

NBA Championship X5

(1998–99, 2002–03, 2004–05, 2006–07, 2013–14)

All-Star Game X15

Season MVP X2

Finals MVP X3

All-NBA First Team X10

All-NBA Second Team X3

All-Defensive First Team X8

All-Defensive Second Team X7

Rookie of the Year X1

EARLY CAREER

Timothy Theodore Duncan was born and raised on the island of Saint Croix, in the US Virgin Islands. He wanted to compete in the sport of swimming and take part in the 1992 Olympics. However, a huge hurricane hit the island and devastated the sporting facility. He was then encouraged to take up basketball.

His college career was characterized by his emotionless and simple personality. He gained many honours at college, and stayed on to finish his degree in psychology, even though there was interest from the NBA. Duncan entered the 1997 draft, and in 1997/98 formed a formidable duo with David Robinson. He played all of the 82 regular games in his rookie season.

LATER CAREER

When his team, the San Antonio Spurs, won the 1999 finals versus the New York Knicks, it was seen as a 'cinderella' story, and a large group came from the Virgin Islands to see their local hero. This was the franchise's first ever NBA championship. The early noughties saw Duncan succeed in scoring and rebounding. He helped his team win the 2003 title and himself the Finals MVP, and with Robinson jointly won the Sports Illustrated 'Sportsmen of the Year' of 2003.

Robinson retired in 2003, but the determined Duncan took on a more authoritative role and helped his team to more titles, including a 4-0 clean sweep of the Cleveland Cavaliers in 2006/07. Knee problems started to hamper him in 2008/09, but in 2010/11 he became the Spurs' all-time points scored and games played record holder. When he completed his 1000th game for the outfit San Antonio had won 707 games and lost only 293 during that time! The 2013/14 season saw a fifth title well into his late 30s, becoming only the second player in history to win the championship in three separate decades. He retired in July 2016 after 19 seasons with the San Antonio Spurs, having attained the most points by a Spurs player in history, and the highest number of victories by a player with just one team in the NBA.

GREATEST ACHIEVEMENTS IN BASKETBALL

Duncan has the remarkable record of having scored at least a point in a game in 1359 consecutive matches. In 1392 games, Duncan managed a total of 26,496 points, 15,091 rebounds (at 10.8 per game), and 4225 assists. He won five championships, three times MVP in Finals, and the Sports Illustrated' Sportsman of the Year. He was voted the NBA Player of the Decade by the same magazine in 2009, and received the Virgin Islands Medal of Honor. He was awarded the Hall of Fame in 2020.

RETIREMENT

Off the court, Duncan briefly took on the role of assistant coach for the Spurs, and also started the 'Tim Duncan Foundation' to help in areas of health, the youth, and education.

SUMMARY

Tim Duncan has been mentioned several times when discussion arises on the greatest power forwards in NBA history. His combined career average in points and rebounds and his defensive statistics are one of the best around. He also played center and his only weakness was the free throw.

KEVIN GARNETT

Full Name	Kevin Maurice Garnett
Nicknames	The Big Ticket
Main Position	Power Forward
Nationality	American
NBA Debut	1995
Height	2.11m, or 6ft 11

CAREER

MINNESOTA TIMBERWOLVES
1995-2007

BROOKLYN NETS
2013-2015

BOSTON CELTICS
2007-2013

MINNESOTA TIMBERWOLVES
2015-2016

TROPHY CABINET

NBA Championship X1
(2007-08)

Season MVP X1

Olympic Gold X1

All-Star Game X15

Rebounds Leader X4

Defensive Player of the Year X1

All-NBA First Team X4

All-NBA Second Team X3

All-Defensive First Team X9

All-Defensive Second Team X3

EARLY CAREER

Born in the city of Greenville, in South Carolina, USA, Kevin Maurice Garnett took a liking to basketball in his school days. He was named the Nation-wide high school player of the year by the high-profile publication, USA Today, having accrued over 2500 points and over 1800 rebounds by the end of his four years at school.

Garnett became one of the few players to actually go to the NBA straight from high school without playing college basketball, in 1995. At 19 years, he was the youngest to join the organization. In 1996/97, he guided the Minnesota Timberwolves to their first ever playoffs. A huge contract signing with the team in 1997 caused many tensions in the league.

LATER CAREER

He led the franchise to a record 58 wins in 2003/04, and saw them reach the playoffs in eight straight seasons. In July 2007, he was traded to the Boston Celtics in exchange for seven players, a league record, having spent his first 12 seasons at Minnesota, with 927 matches already under his belt. He helped the Celtics win the NBA championship in his first season. A year later, he broke the record for being the youngest player in NBA history to compete in a 1000 games at the age of 32. The records kept coming, passing 14,000 rebounds in 2013, and becoming only the third competitor to total a combined 25,000 points, 14,000 rebounds, and 5000 assists in a career.

Garnett returned to Minnesota in 2015 but played only a handful of games due to injury. He then passed Karl Malone's target of the player with the most defensive rebounds in the NBA. He retired in 2016 still wanting to play but was undone in the end by ongoing knee problems.

GREATEST ACHIEVEMENTS IN BASKETBALL

Garnett's 21 seasons in the NBA is tied at second as the most seasons in the league by one individual player. He was on the winning NBA team once, but won several defensive and rebounding awards. He managed 26,071 points at 17.8 per game, and a fantastic 14,662 rebounds at a rate of 10 per game, having played a total of 1462 matches.

He holds a stack of Minnesota Timberwolves franchise records, and is the only NBA player to achieve the combined play stat of 25,000 points, 10,000 rebounds, 5000 assists, 1500 steals, and 1500 blocks in a full career. He won the Olympic Gold in 2000, and was the first to win 'player of the month' four times in one season. His main position was as a 'power forward'.

RETIREMENT

Garnett made his film debut in 2019, was a pundit on television, a consultant, and had an autobiography written in 2021. He also has a minor sharehold in the Italian Serie A soccer club, AS Roma.

SUMMARY

Kevin Garnett will go down in history as one of the best defensive players to compete in the NBA. He had a powerful dunking style and was very intense with a natural athletic ability.

STEPHEN CURRY

Full Name	Wardell Stephen Curry II
Nicknames	Steph, Baby-Faced Assassin
Main Position	Point Guard
Nationality	American
NBA Debut	2009
Height	1.91m, or 6ft 3

CAREER

GOLDEN STATE WARRIORS
2009-2022 (STILL ACTIVE)

TROPHY CABINET

NBA Championship 🏆 X3

(2014-15, 2016-17, 2017-18)

All-Star Game 🏆 X8

Season MVP 🏆 X2

Scoring Leader 🏆 X2

Steals Leader 🏆 X1

All-NBA First Team 🏆 X4

All-NBA Second Team 🏆 X2

EARLY CAREER

Wardell Stephen Curry II was born in the same city as fellow star LeBron James, in Akron, Ohio. He grew up in Charlotte, North Carolina, where his father competed in the NBA. He briefly resided in Toronto, Canada, before achieving success at his high school back in Charlotte. Despite a small frame at the time, Curry climbed to 6 foot 3 by 2007/08, and developed as a point guard. He set the all-time scoring record at his college team, and had a penchant for three-point shooting.

He was selected by the Golden State Warriors in 2009, and by the end of the season, had basketed 30 or more points in eight games, and shot 166 three-point scores, the most by a rookie in the NBA. His brother is also an NBA basketball player.

LATER CAREER

In February 2011, Curry won the Skills Challenge, an event to showcase skills in all facets of the game, and in May, he was honored with the Sportsmanship Award before undergoing surgery on his ankle. The 2012/13 season saw Curry form a potent shooting partnership with Klay Thompson, and by the end of the campaign had become the first player in history to record 300 or more three-pointers in a season, with 314. Along the way, he also became the first to score over 50 points in a game with the aid of at least ten three-pointers.

The staggering numbers just mounted up in the next few years, including the first to basket 400 three-pointers in one season, and six successive seasons of 200+ three-pointers scored. His team, the Golden State Warriors, broke the record for most victories in a season, and won the NBA title three times in four years. Curry was also the fastest to

2000 three-pointers, doing so in 597 games. He missed most of 2019/20 due to a broken hand, but came back to score 96 three-pointers in a month, a new record, before becoming the greatest scorer of three-point goals in NBA history in 2021.

GREATEST ACHIEVEMENTS IN BASKETBALL

With a career still ongoing, Curry has so far won three NBA championships, two MVPs, twice been scoring champion, and twice the three-point contest champ. In 2010 and 2014, he guided the USA to two World Championships. His position is as a 'point guard'.

SUMMARY

Stephen Curry is undoubtedly the best three-point shooter the NBA has ever seen, and has been an advocate of the shot since he made his debut in 2009. From his position of point guard, Curry has excelled in the free throw, stealing, ball handling, and has superb hand-eye coordination. Many teams are forced to double team him to try to contain his scoring, and he has a regular shot range of 30 to 35 feet. Curry has three children, suffers from an eye disorder, is a keen golfer, secured numerous endorsements, and has donated to various charities, including the malaria disease and child-related causes.

BILL RUSSELL

Full Name	William Felton Russell
Nicknames	The Secretary of Defense
Main Position	Center
Nationality	American
NBA Debut	1956
Height	2.06m, or 6ft 9

CAREER

BOSTON CELTICS
1956-1969

TROPHY CABINET

NBA Championship X11

(56-57, 58-59, 59-60, 60-61, 61-62, 62-63, 63-64, 64-65, 65-66, 67-68, 68-69)

All-Star Game X12

Season MVP X5

Rebounds Leader X4

All-NBA First Team X3

All-NBA Second Team X8

All-Defensive First Team X1

Olympic Gold X1

EARLY CAREER

William Felton Russell was born in West Monroe, Louisiana. Racial issues affected his early life, and he lived in poverty when the family moved to Oakland, California. He struggled in his early years as a basketball player finding it difficult to understand the game.

Despite being rejected by college recruits, when he was offered a scholarship he accepted, realising that this was a chance to escape the poverty and racism. His brilliant play saw some rules changed to counteract his dominance. When the Harlem Globetrotters came looking for him he declined their offer and instead he entered the 1956 draft. By the end of the season he took home the title with the Boston Celtics.

LATER CAREER

Russell was instrumental in nurturing Celtics into a potent defensive team to help them gain more success. With Wilt Chamberlain joining up in 1959/60, the Celtics soon registered a record 59 wins in a season, before becoming the first team to register 60 wins in an NBA season in 1961/62. By 1963/64, Celtics had won their sixth consecutive championship, and their seventh overall, in the eight seasons that Russell had been with them. This was the greatest winning streak achieved by any one team in the history of professional US sports competition.

Russell then took up the position of head coach; the first black coach in NBA history. Ten titles in 12 years in 1968, and the exclusive 'Sportsman of the Year' award by the highly admired magazine, Sports Illustrated, was soon followed by 11 in 13 when Russell was aged 35. His prosperous career came to an end in 1969.

GREATEST ACHIEVEMENTS IN BASKETBALL

Russell won the NBA championship an incredible 11 times in his 13 years as a professional. He tied with Henri Richard, an Ice Hockey player, for the most titles won by an individual sportsperson in a North American professional team sports league. He was five times MVP, a rebounding champion, and also a two-time NBA champion as a coach. He was presented with the Presidential Medal of Freedom in 2011, and honoured with the NBA Lifetime Achievement Award in 2019. In 963 games, he achieved an impressive 21,620 rebounds at 22.5 per game, together with over 4000 assists. His position was as a 'center'.

RETIREMENT

In 1971, Russell joined the ABC to do some commentary, and in 1975 was inducted into the Hall of Fame, a ceremony he did not attend. Golf, television hosting, and writing books, were some of the other interests he took up. He had a statue erected in 2013. The MVP for the Finals is now named after him.

SUMMARY

Bill Russell will always be remembered as the man who brought defensive play to the forefront. His main attributes were his shot blocking and rebounding ability, and he showed the importance of defending man-to-man. He is one of the most decorated athletes in North American history, and in 1980 was considered the greatest NBA player ever by the basketball's Writers Association of America.

EARVIN JOHNSON

Full Name	Earvin Johnson Jr.
Nicknames	Magic
Main Position	Point Guard
Nationality	American
NBA Debut	1979
Height	2.03m, or 6ft 8

CAREER

LOS ANGELES LAKERS
1979-1991

LOS ANGELES LAKERS
1995-1996

TROPHY CABINET

NBA Championship X5

(1979-80, 1981-82, 1984-85, 1986-87, 1987-88)

All-Star Game X12

Season MVP X3

Finals MVP X3

Assists Leader X4

Steals Leader X2

All-NBA First Team X9

All-NBA Second Team X1

Olympic Gold X1

EARLY CAREER

Earvin Johnson Jr. was born in the state capital of Michigan, Lansing. He helped his father on the garbage route, and had an interest in basketball at an early age. His favourite player was Bill Russell, and he took the time to practice 'all day'. Both his parents also competed at basketball. He had problems going to high school due to racial problems. The nickname 'magic' was bestowed upon him after a game where he achieved 36 points, 18 rebounds, and 16 assists aged just 15.

Johnson was more interested in concentrating on his studies, but entered the 1979 NBA draft. He was picked by the Los Angeles Lakers, giving him the chance to play with Kareem Abdul-Jabbar. His position was as a point guard in his first season.

LATER CAREER

Having reached the 1980 Finals, an injury to Abdul-Jabbar meant Johnson started game 6 at center. An incredible performance followed, with Johnson recording 42 points, 15 rebounds, seven assists, and three steals to give his side the title, and himself the MVP Finals award, at the end of his first campaign. In 1981, he signed sports' highest paid contract and helped the Lakers to another title in 1982. A series of finals against the Boston Celtics saw Johnson go up against his rival Larry Bird. Johnson came out on top in the 1987 Finals, with his self-proclaimed 'junior....skyhook' the highlight of the win.

The 1988/89 season saw Johnson average 22.5 points and 12.8 assists a game to give him his second MVP prize. After competing in his final championship series in 1991, Johnson was diagnosed with HIV, and immediately announced his retirement. He did compete for the USA team at the 1992 Olympics, winning the gold medal. He was indecisive on whether to return to the game, but used his time off wisely, writing a book, commentating, and taking part in several charitable ventures. He returned as a coach to the Lakers in 1994, and as a player in 1996, aged 36. He retired permanently from the NBA in May 1996.

GREATEST ACHIEVEMENTS IN BASKETBALL

Johnson won the NBA title on five occasions, the MVP in Finals three times, assists and steals awards, and one Olympic gold. He accrued 17,707 points (at 19.5 per game), and 10,141 assists, at a record 11.2 per game. He was a Hall of Fame inductee in 2002, and an NBA Lifetime Achievement award winner in 2019. His position was as a 'point guard'.

RETIREMENT

Since retiring, Johnson started his own team, the 'Magic Johnson All-Stars' which toured around the world, and he had a brief stint in Sweden and Denmark. He became an entrepreneur, a broadcaster, and an advocate on helping to combat the HIV disease. He has also done much work for charitable causes.

SUMMARY

Magic Johnson has been mentioned as probably the best point guard in history, having a superb defensive technique despite his height. He helped introduce 'Showtime' a style of play characterized by fast breaks, speedy passes and accurate feeds.

Printed in Great Britain
by Amazon

83916956R00061